Cirque Press

Copyright ©2023 Ron McFarland

All rights reserved. No part of this publication may be reproduced, distributed or transmitted in any form or by any means, including photocopying, recording, or other electronic or mechanical methods, without the prior written permission of the publisher, except in the case of brief quotations embodied in critical reviews and certain other noncommercial uses permitted by copyright law.

Published by Cirque Press

Sandra Kleven — Michael Burwell

3157 Bettles Bay Loop

Anchorage, AK 99515

Print ISBN:
978-1-7375104-8-2

cirquejournal@gmail.com

www.cirquejournal.com

Cover Art: Georgia Tiffany with Signe Nichols
Author photo: Georgia Tiffany
Book Design: Signe Nichols

A Variable Sense of Things

Ron McFarland

Dedication

For Georgia, of course

and for the Kids:

Kim, Jennifer, Jon

and for the Grandkids:

Sara, Mia & Spencer, Kaiden & Natalie

and for the Other Grandkids:

Isaiah, Katherine & Nick, Billy

Acknowledgments

Poems in this collection previously appeared in the following magazines and have in some cases been slightly altered: *491 Magazine, Aura Literary Arts Review, Cape Rock, Chautauqua, Cirque, Concho River Review, Dappled Things, Dunes Review, Front Range Review, Illuminations, Lost Coast Review, Naugatuck Review, New Madrid, Pinyon, Raven Chronicles, Rockford Review, Slant, Spitball, Talking River Review, Triggerfish Critical Review, Visions International, Whitefish Review, Wilderness House Literary Review, Xavier Review.*

Special thanks to Bob Wrigley for sustaining me in the craft and to Mike Burwell for shaping up this otherwise sprawling collection!

Contents

I.

The Prayers of Seeds . . . 8
Poems Lovely as Trees . . . 9
Timber Grain Elevators . . . 10
Piano Lessons: Danny, Age 6, Masters the Circle of Fifths . . . 11
The Mad Teacher . . . 12
Welcome to Junior High . . . 13
Vocational Education . . . 14
Artificial Respiration . . . 16
Protected Species . . . 17
The Preacher's Kid . . . 18
Near Manatee Cove . . . 20
Elegy of the Bottlenose Dolphin . . . 21
Lament at the County Fair . . . 22
At the Carnival . . . 23
Transfiguration . . . 24
What Our Mother Couldn't Throw Away . . . 25
Pretty Bird . . . 26

II.

The Character of Place . . . 30
The Outliers Among Us . . . 32
Hanna Coal Co., Mine #10 . . . 33
At Stoney's Service Station . . . 34
Rojek's . . . 35
Small-Town Patriot . . . 36
The Psychopoetics of Everyday Life . . . 38
The Librarian's Family . . . 39
Entitlements . . . 40
The Romance of Logging . . . 41
Customer Service Representative . . . 42
Therapy Pool . . . 44

III.

Eco-Workout . . . 48
The Frustrations of Horticulture . . . 49
The World's Worst Catholic . . . 50
My Favorite Deadly Sin . . . 51
Animal Sympathy . . . 53
About Rabbits . . . 54
Your Social Security Number . . . 56
Too Late, Too Early . . . 57
Not Welcome . . . 58
Today I Decide Not to Write about the Vanishing Snow Leopards . . . 59
Vespula pennsylvanica, the Western Yellowjacket . . . 60
Guided Tour of the Hemingway Home and Museum . . . 62
Papa Visits the Key West Place . . . 64
Find a Grave . . . 66
Citizens of the World . . . 68
In October . . . 70
My Brother's War . . . 71
Lessons from the War: The Forgetting of Parts . . . 72
Language Barriers . . . 74
Poems for "The Hurting Kind" . . . 76
Marking Papers While Watching a Baseball Game . . . 78

IV.

Don't Feed the Bears . . . 80
The Lover of Lakes . . . 82
Arachnophilia . . . 84
At the Speed of Love . . . 85
A Lover's Game . . . 86
The Photographer & the Angler . . . 87
Aquariums . . . 88
Amish Furniture in Sequim, Washington . . . 89
Romance on the Patio . . . 91
Backyard Bird Count . . . 92

I.

The Prayers of Seeds

We who would be root, who would
delve into the darkness of dirt,
who would slenderly upthrust ourselves
green into the photosynthetic sun,
who would toughen in the variable
air, who would rise and fall
simultaneously, who would spread
ourselves in all directions, who would
leaf out laughing though heard
by no one, who would furl up
into buds and burst into blooms
to await the coming of bees,
who would carry bits of us away,
in a manner of speaking, who would
be converted (hallelujah!) into some
heavenly substance, who would
wither and be transfigured into
tiny dry miracles of ourselves, we pray.

Poems Lovely as Trees

Teacher told them each to write a poem on trees.
Some of them wrote with a vengeance
born of the fear of parental censure,
some from a sense of quiet desperation,
many on impulse, a few from love,
though not so often the love of words.

Teacher told them to illustrate their work.
They must use their imagination.
They must do their best to think
like specific trees: think like an oak,
like a maple shedding its leaves, like larch,
white pine, willow beside a slow stream.

Teacher told them they must reach high,
walked them around the block for inspiration.
Natalie pinched Kaiden and made him cry.
Mia slapped Ben because she really liked him.
Spencer said nothing because he secretly loved
Lily and Mia. Then it started to rain. Hard.

Teacher told them she would have their poems
displayed at the county fair so everyone
could see and admire. They must do their best.
Trees soon swept over their fourth-grade world
like skyscrapers in nine out of thirty-six poems.
The judge awarded each one a blue ribbon.

Timber Grain Elevators

It took so long to disassemble that old
grain elevator near Belmont we thought
it might just go ahead and tumble down
under the weight of its bad memories.

This one was built around nineteen-twenty,
cribbed two-by-sixes tapered to fours laid
flat for durability. Some tourists ask
who lived in the headhouse there on top.

We have to laugh. But folks hereabouts
sometimes worry ghosts from bad crop years
haunt the skeleton, ghosts that grumble
about wheat prices tumbling, grain trains

backed up in Spokane, ghosts of those
two workers who fell in back in the Thirties.
Some farmers claim the wood absorbs moisture
better than concrete, but the insurance boys

don't see it that way, so some guys began
dismantling them to salvage the wood.
That one near Belmont was a beaut, but
haunted for sure, as they'll soon find out.

Piano Lessons: Danny, Age 6, Masters the Circle of Fifths

Only the most talented and most disciplined
among them will move on and when they move on
they will forget her or perhaps remember her
only as that Mrs. Someone they took from
their first year or two when they were five or six.

Yesterday she heard her neighbor tell the boy
who helps her with the yard she wouldn't need him
today. Wouldn't need him. That, she thinks, is how it
feels to have been, but now not to be, needed.

When she was twelve she placed second in the Spokane
piano competition against seventeen-year-olds.
When she was sixteen Van Cliburn played Brahms
on her Steinway, that one right there in the living-room

where she still teaches once or twice a week, four or five
young ones. It depends. But even the best lack her discipline,
or talent, though she was never, her mother would say,
fully accomplished. Times change. She still loves the piano
and teaching, but the best of them do move on.

The Mad Teacher

The teacher went mad so slowly
only her best students would know
when to applaud.
Her fellow teachers, even the coaches,
just thought
she was acting odd,
and the rest of her students
laughed when the best ones laughed
and tried not to stare at the clock too hard.

She began to alternate her dresses,
pale blue and faded gray,
and she had her hair cut short and then
ignored it altogether.
She began to wear the same sweater
regardless of the weather.
Her better students noticed the stains,
the torn seam on the left sleeve,
but they were polite.

Some days she'd say "good-night"
or "Hemingway," meaning to say
"misplaced modifier,"
but even her worst students understood,
and the best caught fire.
Once she filed her lunch under T
for tuna, and that made a mess,
but all her students scored well
on the standardized tests.

Welcome to Junior High

Remember when you got along
so well with others?
Remember how you
never needed improvement?
Well, that was before seventh grade
cowboy, cowgirl, cowpoke.

Now you feel more like a cow.
Now you've found yourself
in seventh grade section four,
realm of the indifferent,
world of the uncertain universe
of where do you go from here?

Your would-be girlfriend
has turned up in section one
along with the boy who will soon
morph into the quarterback,
the power forward, the striker
on the soccer team, the boy who

sprints the hundred, plays chess
like a junior grand master.
But at least you didn't get stuck
in section nine, right? So, where
do you think you might be going
from here?

Vocational Education

"Every kid needs a calling."

Back then, and never mind when
that was, guys planning not
to go to college, even junior college,
took shop at CHS and learned
how to do things, how to make things,
and while I struggled with algebra,
Stanley Yates and John Ramsey
studied the applied physics of the
internal combustion engine and the
chemistry of oil, gas, and battery acid.

One semester they took woodworking,
operating a lathe, creating lamps
out of cypress knees, building
sturdy bookcases for the Chilton's
auto repair manuals they'd read
in favor of *To Kill a Mockingbird,*
Pride and Prejudice, and *Macbeth.*

Decades later John and Stan knew
all about timing, all about how things
work, or ought to work, and if it wasn't
right, they'd make it right, or you
wouldn't have to pay a dime for what
you didn't know a thing about.

John made his wife a table and chairs
out of walnut so fine-grained you'd want to
stroke it as if it were a purebred hound.
Stan never married. In his spare time

he built birdhouses that looked like
mansions or, for mockingbirds,
plain, sturdy structures using cedar,
sometimes dogwood. Florida's state bird.

My only attempt at woodworking
was a simple planter: five scraps of
random lumber sawed and tacked
into a lopsided rectangular box that
proved not fit for much of anything.
My wife says she loves it,
claims it looks too elegant for dirt.

Artificial Respiration

How long? we asked our thin
preadolescent muscles as they
strained against the back
of a friend pretending to die.

Those were the easy days
of back-pressure, arm-lift.
We counted one elephant, two
elephants, maybe kangaroos.

We were busy being prepared,
good Boy Scouts earning
merit badges by pretending
to save a human life.

In real life we knew
we'd never have to do this.
How soon we grew tired.
How soon our arms ached.

How long? we asked Mr. Phelps.
As long as it takes, he said.
Then he muttered softly,
sometimes longer.

Protected Species

As Florida boys we saw no manatees,
only sea cows galumphing along the lagoons
or lolling unpresumptively
keeping their gray lumpish profiles
free of mermaid analogies.
These clumsy vegetarians, part fish
part mammal, we were told
were gentle creatures, early Eocene,
known for their long-term memories.
We thought of course of elephants,
but Mr. Kline, our science teacher,
claimed manatees were mostly loners,
claimed they slept half the day
mostly upside down and grazed the rest.
They simply swam or bumped or oozed along.
We never witnessed them stampede.
Now we wish devoutly they would
get a move on, plow their way out of here,
escape the speedboats, red tide, algae bloom,
whatever doom we've stored up for them.
Nigerian guy who played left wing for us
claimed the Yoruba believed
manatees were human once and much,
much better behaved.

The Preacher's Kid

At about age twelve, I spent the night
at our preacher's house, technically the manse,
next door to the First Presbyterian Church
of Rockledge, Florida, on the banks of the lovely
Indian River, technically a lagoon,
because his son Julian (they were new in town)
was kind of a friend, technically a vague
acquaintance from Sunday school and junior high
band where he played squeaky clarinet
that matched the blat of my brassy cornet.

The house was one of those white stucco affairs
built in the nineteen-twenties boom,
and Julian's room, where he showed me a small
glass jar filled with his baby teeth,
was on the second floor, warm and not air-conditioned.
I did not encourage him to open the jar but felt
vaguely relieved when he just gave it a shake
and placed it back on the shelf. I did not
tell him in school the cool kids called him
"Juliana Pauline Wellers," his middle name
being Paul. I don't recall what we had for dinner.

But the strangest thing about him,
it seemed to me then: he was a bird-watcher,
technically, I guess, an amateur ornithologist,
binoculars and all. Of course I told no one.
After all, what would the cool kids think of me?

This morning, sixty years later, I thought of that stay
because yesterday I got a copy of the *Audubon Magazine*
in the mail because last month I made a donation,
not that I've ever been a bird-watcher,
except down the barrel of my 12-gauge Remington,
but because it seemed such a worthy cause.
So there I was flipping the glossy pages
and thinking of Julian Wellers counting the birds

in Brevard County, alone in the mangrove swamps
with those binoculars jotting down mockingbirds,
bobwhite quail, great blue heron, brown pelican,
mallard, coot, pintail, seagulls, cinnamon teal,
bufflehead, loon, cormorant, flamingo, osprey,
snakebird, technically anhinga, turkey buzzard,
kestrel, cardinal, blue jay, red-tailed hawk,
sandpiper, least tern, roseate spoonbill,
mourning dove, downy woodpecker, indigo bunting,
at least a dozen species of warblers, you get the picture.

Julian camps under the arboreal scourge of Florida,
the invasive Brazilian pepper-tree
decked out with its bright red toxic berries,
and tabulates more avian species than he has
teeth in his jar back at the parsonage,
technically manse, the perfect preacher's kid.
Today, who knows, a jazz musician perhaps,
a Presbyterian minister, a prosperous orthodontist.

On page fifty of the magazine a peregrine falcon
flies toward the crease, its bright yellow talons
gripping the neck of a willet whose gray beak
parts in a shriek that can only mean one thing.

Near Manatee Cove

> *They do not spout.*
> — Herman Melville

The sight of scars across the dark
bristly backs of these docile creatures
alarmed us a bit. Then our kids
started to bring their drawings home

from school, herds of smiling sea cows,
gentle herbivores gliding along our
improbably blue Indian River Lagoon.
"Lumbering," mothers said. "Lovably ugly."

Awkward and slow, no wonder they
couldn't escape the props of our
pleasure boats cutting their way
through channels, across canals.

We thought placing no-wake signs
at Humpback Bridge on Sykes Creek
might do the job. Making it stick
on the Barge Canal worked for a while.

Until it seemed, quite unpredictably,
the seagrass vanished as if overnight.
Who would've guessed aside from
marine biologists and saltwater anglers?

But who listens to those angry blokes,
eco-troublemakers, eco-maniacs?
Emaciated manatees by the dozens
starved seeking a nice place to die.

Elegy of the Bottlenose Dolphin

We deem ourselves more beautiful by far
and smarter than our chunky porpoise cousins,
but it's not their snub-nosed corpses that reek
and clutter the coast from Chokoloskee Bay
north to Tarpon Springs where each year fewer
sponge divers descend to the floor of the Gulf,
but ours.

Where the Caloosahatchee seeps in slowly,
guacamole-green these days, the twirling
dinoflagellates tint the waters with
decadent palettes. *Karenia brevis*
contributes its ominous red bloom,
cloudy from a distance and almost
beautiful.

For decades we've amused you with our play
(if you don't remember *Flipper,* look it up).
We communicate in merry chirps and squeaks.
If we could speak your language, understand
your neurotoxins, how they affect your brain,
we could perhaps explain you
to yourselves.

Lament at the County Fair

Most of my songs are sad
but I'm a happy person,
believe me, except perhaps
when writing my songs
or singing them.

Haven't you seen me on stage
at the county fair in September
singing sadly, strumming my
old guitar? When I stop
no one applauds.

Maybe I'm drowned out by
shouts from the Ferris Wheel,
shrieks from the Gravitron,
lowing 4-H cows, bleating sheep
about to be meat.

Believe me, I take none of this
personally because I sing for all,
for clucking hens and mute rabbits,
for raucous children and silent adults.

At the Carnival

By the glare of naked bulbs rowed up
to throw the eyes
away from the soiled hands
of the man at the ring toss game,
I saw, at the age of thirteen, my father
by a different light.
Strangely, as if in a dream, he fished
dollars from his worn wallet
chasing a portable radio
while my mother stood
quivering in angry tears
when the carnie
raised his grimy fingers
glittering with thick false diamonds
above the counter.
The next ring plopped over a peg
with a pocketknife, Dad's prize.
I have it still with its almost mother-of-pearl
handle and its two dull blades.
I saw at age thirteen my father
shrug his shoulders at the clattering carnival
while his hardware store
quietly went under back in town,
and my mother complained the last thing
we needed was a portable radio,
and my father calmly explained
we all have our limits.

Transfiguration

In a snapshot I've not visited in many years,
my mother sits waist deep in the Atlantic
at Cocoa Beach, wet-framed by the spray
of a sudden wave.
      In my vague memory
she's wearing a pink swimsuit and she's
laughing as if she's not afraid of the water.
She cannot swim.
      In the Ohio coal towns
where she grew up, the streams still flow
bright orange. In the nearby muddy ponds
her brothers would jump in on humid
summer afternoons and dogpaddle back
to where she sat
      alone and watching and scared.
When we moved to Florida, frightened as ever,
our mother signed us up for swimming lessons
first thing. My brother and I took to it
like gleeful ducks but heeded her advice
not to go out too far.
      Somehow Dad's camera
that surprising afternoon managed to transform
her fear into something like unpredictable
delight. Somehow our mother terrified us
into being smart.

What Our Mother Couldn't Throw Away

For instance, that tiny vial of orange perfume
shaped like an oil lamp with a red plastic
chimney my brother and I bought at Kresge's
and which she would never open,
she said, because ordinary air
might spoil the fragrance.
She kept it enshrined there
on her dresser till we forgot all about it.

And of course, I recall that misshaped
blue lump of kiln-fired clay that well
might've served as an ashtray
had Mom been a smoker, which she wasn't.
How did it make its way back
from vague memory into my possession?
After she passed, Dad sent what he called
"a box of things your mother kept."

Not among them the imitation ivory plastic
heart-shaped ring box Dad drew from his
khakis to propose that icy Ohio day
about the time Hitler's Wehrmacht bogged down
in the snows of Stalingrad.
Later that year Dad wrote his only poem
from an antiaircraft battery in Washington, DC,
gilt-framed now on our sister's dresser in Florida.

Pretty Bird

Hemingway wrote the most important thing
for a writer to have is an unhappy
childhood. Sadly, mine proved joyous,
my family so much in sync we believed
our green parakeet kept repeating
"pretty bird, pretty bird"
throughout my boyhood.
Bippy, we agreed, was year-round cheerful.

Charged with cleaning Bippy's cage,
laying out newspaper, measuring
water, dispensing fresh birdseed,
my brother and I proved less cheery.
We tried to teach him a bit of light
profanity: "Say 'shit-shit-shit,'" we said.
But that good Presbyterian bird,
would have none of it.

Who needed this bird, my brother asked?
No one seemed to know. We speculated
Bippy was meant to teach us how to be
responsible citizens, empathetic,
eager members of the congregation
singing in the choir,
caring adults-in-process.
But neither of us could carry a tune.

One afternoon when I came home from school,
Mom was sitting on the porch waiting for me,
nursing her girlish phobia: fear of birds.
Bippy'd gotten loose, surely my brother's
doing, and now was soaring about the house

pretty-bird-free and doubtless
singing his tiny heart out.
When I popped open the door, off he flew,

to propagate a flock of green or blue
parakeets cheeping "pretty bird, pretty bird"
or possibly "shit-shit-shit"
from Cocoa Beach to Key West.

II.

The Character of Place

Well, it's got to happen somewhere, right?
And Hemingway says there's got to be
weather in the damned thing. In the supreme
fiction it's where these particular people must be.
They find themselves, almost surprisingly, stuck.

Consider Chekhov's characters and just like that:
Russia somewhere, somewhere in Russia
and likely the nineteenth century at that,
late, or early in the twentieth. They're stuck
with Tsar Nicholas and probably bad weather.
It all happened in the village of N _____.
But really, what are we to do with that?

Give us, at least dear Anton, a muddy road
and an ill-tempered peasant, probably drunk.
Vodka of course, cheap vodka, tsarist rotgut.
That helps. A drab and dirty little tavern then
in the village of N _____. It's April
and the small redbud's struggling to bloom.
Maybe it's the only tree in town? Ridiculous.

Let's give this story a much more Russian
tree or shrub, something unlikely to show up
in southern Ohio, and why have just the one?
Let's say everyone's wearing black or gray.
It's Russia, okay? Eighteen-ninety or so, maybe
nineteen-o-one, before color came to the provinces.

A cold wind blows up, tortures the dry grass.
Old Semyon misses his daughter Olga who lives
far away in Minsk. Chekhov needs to get him
into the tavern so Mikhail Ivanovich can buy him
a couple shots of bad vodka; therefore, a few icy
snowflakes suddenly bluster in from the west.

That does it. Now he's inside and the coal oil lamp
sputters in the gathering darkness and the bartender
ignores him pointedly because his in-laws
are visiting from Moscow for two months.
Old Semyon has grown hungry but there's nothing
but pickled herring and he hates pickled herring.

Mikhail comes over and buys him a shot of vodka,
bad vodka, and then another. Gradually, where they are
doesn't matter much. The character of place fades.
Even the weather doesn't matter all that much in this
nasty tavern on the great broad Steppes of Russia.

The Outliers Among Us

Amy's chickens clucking across the street
remind my father of old Pete Murchison,
Neffs, Ohio, nineteen-thirties mining town,
how old Pete liked to roam around
crowing like a rooster at odd hours.

Hearing his story reminds me of Henry,
a hulking man of indeterminate age
and very few words whose vocation
appeared to be offering a single rose
to random coeds. Known to be harmless,
he was said to be the only son of old
Tallahassee money, the twice-great grandson
of a Confederate major killed at Shiloh.

Every town should tolerate at least one
such oddball, one such human who eschews
what ordinary mortals think makes sense.
Here, it's a lady named Helen who wears
aluminum foil inside her pith helmet
and frequently clenches a dinner fork
between her teeth to deflect radiation.
Some say she's a genius, a mad botanist.
She knows the whereabouts of morels
and huckleberries. The rest of us just guess.

Hanna Coal Co., Mine #10
Neffs, Ohio, March 16, 1940

You need to see this place in the murk
of early November, after Halloween and
well before Thanksgiving. No snow that day,
only a loitering grayness everywhere.

Coal miners made good but dangerous pay,
spoke in broken English, myriad accents.
Locals called them bohunks, or hunkies,
even the ones from Italy or Wales.

Some of them nurtured dreams of working at
Wheeling Steel or one of the glass factories.
They talked about that while shooting pool
at Tony's over schooners of ten cent beer.

Next day they trooped to the bituminous
pits at Willow Grove, one of the Polacks
telling what happened to a cousin in Warsaw
the year before: "Don't never go to war."

The mine blew on the verge of spring
as willows were beginning to yellow up and
seventy-two men found themselves reduced
suddenly to a small, gray, marble monument.

At Stoney's Service Station

"Be Sure with Pure" had surely a ring to it
its successor, Union 76, does not, but
when the station switched brands and two
brothers back from the Korean War took over,
that's what they got, along with racy calendars
from a local auto body shop that featured
less than half-dressed ladies their big sister
would not have liked.
                           In the Men's Room
boys and grandfathers scrubbed their paws
with Lava soap, charcoal gray and coarse,
containing ground pumice meant for
hands that would know just what to make
of those fleshy, heavy breasted women
who knew erotically different ways to
celebrate every month from frigid January
through sunny May and into the torrid
summer months of masculine adolescence
and on to the autumns of their discontent
that haunt them still as winters threaten.

Rojek's

What would it have been like to have lived
above that mom-and-pop's grocery in Cocoa,
where Pineda hit Peachtree, where I delivered
the *Tribune* Monday, Wednesday, and Friday afternoons
culminating in the smell of overripe bananas?

The Rojeks, rumored to have left Poland just in
time's nick—Henry behind the meat counter,
always guarded, his cleaver at the ready—
Marta, his overly bosomed wife,
running the register and peeling her eyes

for boys like me who clearly lusted for
penny candy and bubblegum baseball cards.
Those were the days of Mickey Mantle,
Yogi Berra, Stan Musial, Ted Williams,
Ted Kluszweski, heroes with hundreds of faces.

The place was not air-conditioned, the fans
lackluster, indifferent to the big league
humidity, and where the Rojeks lived,
over the rows of Campbell's soup, Del Monte
green beans, wilting lettuce and shriveled apples,
heat accumulated all day every day.
To them it must have felt like safety.

Small-Town Patriot

July Fourth, small-town Idaho, finds me
riding in the back of a '39 Dodge pickup
tossing candy to random kids
(I'm from elsewhere) and their overly
tattooed parents, half of whom,
I speculate, are hooked on meth.
Their teeth look gray, and like I said,
I'm from somewhere else.

Larry, fighting the oversized steering wheel,
beeps his horn, which sounds like
sheep bleating about peace in our time.
I've given out of sweets halfway
through town. I'm greeted with frowns
despite my star-spangled plastic top hat
under which I am copiously sweating.
Clearly, I'm from elsewhere.

Larry has promised a great pulled pork
barbecue served up by the local 4-H
along with watermelon and homemade
chocolate chip cookies, but no beer.
That's for later, he says, on the porch
back at his dwindling dairy farm.

Desperate to prove myself patriotic,
worthy of my Eagle Scout achievement
sixty years back, I rise from my folding chair
and do my best to imitate Jimmy Cagney
imitating George M. Cohan tapping and singing,

"I'm a Yankee Doodle dandy,
A Yankee Doodle do or die."
I'm from way, way out of town,
and I am all out of candy.

The Psychopoetics of Everyday Life

The news in this town is that there's no news
including the overweight waitress at The Hilltop
who's known everyone here all her inescapable life.
Name's Amy.
            Every farmer and rancher around town
comes here to kickstart his long day over biscuits
like Amy's grandmother used to make and gravy.
Someone's little girl was running a hundred and two
so they took her over to Doc Blanchard's
and (thank you guys)
                 someone else's daughter's
gone off to college and God knows she won't be back.
(Oh, yes she will.
            She'll be back, you can count on it.)
Them deer's eatin' near everthing in the wife's garden
and's workin' on the flowers and shrubs now.
One of 'em run into Oscar's old pickup last week
when it was snowin' to beat Pete's pig
(have a good day)
              messed it up good and didn't do
that big old buck much good neither. Filled his freezer.
Says it sounded like a hand grenade when it hit.
(What's old Oscar know what a hand grenade
sounds like?)
           Gifford's boy's talking about
joining the army again—that little Lisa just about
broke his heart. He was a pretty fair country quarterback.
Beth was all achy and everything, couldn't get back
to sleep.
         Whatever it is, I'll be getting it next.
Well, there's something bad going around for sure.
(How was your breakfast, honey?)

The Librarian's Family

Small town anywhere, marginal library
(no one checks out books nowadays,
hunkering over computers instead),
librarian's husband does mechanic work
at the John Deere place and beers his way
one day to the next, reads nothing but
technical manuals, dips Copenhagen,
their son flailing his way through high school
thanks to football, their daughter dropped out
years back and moved off, calls now and then
to beg for a loan, says she's drowning,
says she's in Hell, do her parents know,
do her parents even have a clue?
Her mother says she believes she does.

Entitlements

Four large gray spools of hay
tumbled from the snowy hillside
rest at the edge of the road
above Kendrick, Idaho,
as if some irate giant decided
the stuff would never sell
and shoved it over,
hoping in some vague way
to collect on crop insurance
because the wife bailed in July
and now wants child support
and his mom down in Boise has
gone bonkers and needs to be
put someplace and who the hell
can afford that given the damn
transmission give out on him
last week and him a good thirty
years out from social security?

The Romance of Logging

Artless, blurred black-and-white films
document old growth stands falling,
crumpling to the forest floor
in clouds of dust and duff and roar,
and a dirty-faced, whiskery lumberjack
grins and yells "timber!" Glorious work.

Bull pine, hemlock, tamarack,
western cedar, spruce and fir, any tree
worth anything must drop like destiny
and then be shot down flumes to crash
into the river where cork-boot loggers
wield their peaveys like spears and execute
dangerous dance steps on the tumbling
limbless trees. Glorious conquest.

No wonder young punks drop out of school
(even the football coach can't stop them)
to trim limbs for a couple of years
and set chokers in fond hopes the cheerleaders
will take notice. The smart ones don't.
The others get pregnant and drop out of school.

The timber punks grow up and develop
a taste for Copenhagen, and never mature.
Laid off, maybe they'll take their chances
pulling green chain down at the mill,
locally owned, long hours of racket and splinters,
maybe a lost thumb, backache, red beer after work,
loud music, not a cheerleader in the joint.

Customer Service Representative

At the credit union where I sit all day
at my dull computer, a Dell,
flashing my radiant smile and thinking
about my weight, I work hard
to focus on other things:
the bloated accounts of certain depositors,
my own slim savings, my ex back in Denver.

How could this have happened to me?
All my life I've nourished such
slender dreams, such slight desires.
But oh! my peaches-and-cream complexion,
my dark and fiery eyes.

Examining my neatly manicured nails,
I think how Mother always insisted,
"it's what's inside that counts."
Where I have my nails done,
Eileen tells me I'm just fleshy,
sensual the way the Old Masters liked:
Rembrandt, Titian, Rubens.

If my mother knew what I paid
for these exquisitely enameled nails,
she'd have croaked.
Big Mike, my ex, liked
plump chicks, he claimed, up to a point.
He played o-line for the Buffalos
until his knees gave out. Now, I always
root against the Broncos, his fantasy team.

Outside, wind blows thin branches
from an old birch. I smile when they snap.
My dark eyes light up for this client,
short guy, world's cutest optometrist.
Feeling powerfully full-bodied, I
stroke my silk-smooth cheek with my
eloquently tapered fingers. I might
start taking piano lessons again.
Mother would like that.

Therapy Pool

The arthritic ladies wait in the pool
for Odette, their lithe instructor,
meticulous, firm, almost kind some days.
Her difficult job weighs on her.

When Odette swam competitively,
butterfly her best stroke, one afternoon
she broke the school record
and placed at state but didn't win.
Now she will not allow herself
to think about old dreams.
Simply getting the names straight
one day to the next seems to be enough:
who they are and who they once were.

Gail the mathematician laughs
but cannot hold a piece of chalk
long enough for anything to add up.
Joanne the legislator's wife
cannot uproot the loosestrife
that threatens her poppies
there on the corner of Third and Blaine.

And Betty, or was it Brenda,
Odette always gets them confused,
used to knit afghans for every baby
born to her sprawling brood.
Now her fingers gnarl like old roots.
And Brenda, or Betty,
whichever one's left, once
played on the Steinway at Carnegie Hall.

But maybe it's all made up, those once
remarkable, now arthritic, lives.
"Just wave your fingers sideways
through the water, ladies," Odette instructs,
"as if you were waving goodbye."

III.

Eco-Workout

Stepping aboard the ellipticals
I switch channels from politics
to nature, where a northern harrier
swoops on a burrow of prairie dogs,
coming up empty, and then a coyote
lopes past in broad daylight
opting not to waste his time.

The camera catches these rodents
yipping warnings to each other as if,
even there in the desert, community
could mean security when along
slithers an eight-foot bull snake,
hungry for lunch, and papa
prairie dog begins to hop and yip,
distracting the famished constrictor
from his clutch of innocent pups.

I'm working up a healthy sweat
getting nowhere fast and I think,
"Nature bloody in tooth and claw."
Not to mention the fatal embrace
of an ethically neutral snake.
Nature must be served, I tell myself.
But what if children are watching,
or, may the gods help us, a passel of
innocent pols down at the statehouse?

The Frustrations of Horticulture

Planted a struggle of garden where
radishes shriveled beneath the soil,
turned wooden, sprouted pale
blue flowers in mockery, where
two fat rabbits ambled through
one evening and devoured the
delicate green promises of Bibb
lettuce and Black Seeded Simpson,
where tomatoes waited green and hard
until way too late even to be
dipped in cornmeal and fried,
where tiny red larvae
dined voraciously on the turnips.
Planted it all to strawberries
and marigolds the next year.
Every bird in the neighborhood
celebrated the strawberries.
They say mosquitoes hate marigolds.
Not these mosquitoes.

The World's Worst Catholic

In the home of the world's worst Catholic
you will find no crucifixes,
no hope of repelling vampires,
no sacred flaming heart of Mary
mother of god whose name must go
uncapitalized in the name of equity.

In the home of the world's worst Catholic
no one hopes Gonzaga makes it
again to the Big Dance or that Notre Dame
sashays into the Top Ten in football,
no one confuses Xavier with Xanadu
or Holy Cross with holy cow!

In the home of the world's worst Catholic
no one confesses, no one atones
for their sins or agrees to own
a single one of them, no one reads
Dante's *Divine Comedy*, but everyone
takes Milton's *Paradise Lost* to heart.

No one prays the rosary, mumbles
"Ave Maria" or "Pater Noster" in that
long forgotten Latin mumbo-jumbo
litany, no one lights candles in memory
because no one suffers the nostalgia of regret
in the home of the world's worst Catholic.

My Favorite Deadly Sin

> *And eke the verse of famous Poets witt*
> *He does backbite, and spightfull poison spues*
> *From leprous mouth on all, that ever writt.*
> — Spenser, Faerie Queene I.iv.32

In my most envious dream, I pretend
not to ride a ravenous wolf in your
homecoming parade, tickertape
decorating your victorious shoulders.
Reading whatever you've written lately
turns me inside out
(remember the playground line—
into sauerkraut),
so I've shelved you, left you
dangling like a forgotten participle.
In my most envious dream, you need this
lack of adulation.
                    You'll be a better man
for this sham felicitation, and I will
find out other foods to chew
besides those venomous toads
that keep cropping up in my bibliography.
I've learned to avoid your website,
full-color photographs, you and your
more than satisfactory wife
and unbelievably happy children.
How did you contrive to make them
rhyme so well with success?
In my most envious dream, I confess,
you die miserably as I lick a malicious
root beer popsicle. My best dreams
work like this.
              In my chest I nourish a nest,

make that a feast, of secretive vipers. We get along.
I keep hoping you'll drop by for coffee.
We can talk about your latest,
and I can introduce you to my favorite
slithering pets.

Animal Sympathy

> *Please, No Animals*
> — (sign at a Seattle hotel)

What if you don't like to read
about horses and dogs,
not even in poems?
What if you can't stand the way
they whinny and neigh,
bark, yap, and whine
line after line
trying to wheedle their animal plight
into your preciously human mind?

You know they can't mean
anything by it, right,
despite what some poets indite?
Meaning's a function of language
and frontal lobes,
that sort of thing.
But how, you ask, do they sing?
Well, doggies and horsies
don't sing—they don't even think.

They just stare at us,
mindlessly glare at us
till we lead ourselves to the brink
of thinking they think.
And then we will their affection,
force it
like unwanted sex.
So, what do you think of that?
No. Don't even mention your cat.

About Rabbits

> *And to feel that the light is a rabbit-light.*
> — Wallace Stevens

My wife says she can remember almost
every rabbit story she ever heard:
the Velveteen Rabbit, the Easter Bunny,
Peter Rabbit, Peter Cottontail hopping
down the bunny trail, Uncle Wiggly,
the pink Energizer Bunny beating its
non-stop drum, Br'er Rabbit and his
kindred spirit Bugs outsmarting everyone.

The world's overrun with these prey animals
that could make temporary pets or decent
dinners. Consider the blood-stained highways
of Nevada, southern Idaho, Wyoming.
Jackrabbits may be the dumbest of bunnies.
My first-grade girlfriend would stuff her slim
cold fingers into a little white muff in Ohio
never considering its tragic origins.

Someone said bunnies breed like Greek gods,
lying on their backs and whining ecstatically.
One afternoon I emptied my twelve-gauge
at a furry gray flash off Coyote Grade.
They taste great stewed, but you must
hit one first, and one afternoon at elk camp
Rick got lucky and we roasted the critter
on a spit over an open campfire.

But then we drank so much beer and
Jägermeister, we forgot all about that
unlucky snowshoe hare, and it ended up
tasting not like chicken but about like
you might think old rawhide might taste.
My wife, who prides herself on keeping
the world's greatest gardens, always
plants a row or two for the rabbits.

Your Social Security Number

Late in April you get this message from the IRS
claiming some hacker may have impersonated you
to the tune of ten G's using your social
apparently insecurity number toward that
insidious end.
                    So, an agent calls and you have
this long chat, and he seems a swell enough
fellow and seems to believe you're almost
exactly who you claim to be, but after seven months
with no refund, you're starting to wonder just who you are
and about that slut,
                    your apparently promiscuous
social security number. Scott, your accountant, says
not to worry, everyone knows her anyway, and he seems
a swell enough fellow, a good Rotarian
and an upstanding middle-aged Presbyterian
to boot.
            But see how it is? She's been with you
all these years, and now you're seeing her in an
entirely different light, as if for the first time,
naked in some voluptuous spa in Las Vegas,
and you're here to say
                    you've never even been to Vegas.
Scott used to drive an ambiguous Buick,
but last week you spotted him behind the wheel of a new
Mercedes E63, damn the gas mileage, and that
sleek lady leaning back on the full-grain Napa leather,
yeah, you know who she is.

Too Late, Too Early

That box of chicken broth in the fridge
features a "best by" date two years past.

You try so hard to keep yourself up to date,
to stay on top of any and every thing

that this business with the chicken broth
nags you past midnight, makes you think

maybe you don't deserve a good night's rest,
let alone sleep. This is what it means,

you suspect, to grow old, to be a few
uncertain years past your best ones.

Maybe, you think, as you drowse off, or not,
no one will notice and you'll answer the phone

cheerily "good morning" as if you meant it
only to hear a man's foreign voice pleading

for a donation to yet another worthy cause
because where he's calling from it's not

six o'clock a.m. and he's wide awake
and though he doesn't say so wonders
what can possibly be wrong with you?

Not Welcome

Spent too much time this morning
watching a squirrel negotiate
our feeder by the patio.

How desperate was he to get
more than we think he needs?
Good Mr. Nutkin, good American.

Go for it. Go for my suburban
lifestyle symbol, my Audubon
squirrel-proof bird feeder

equipped with my ingenious baffle
contrived to keep you distant,
where you belong, in some other,

less desirable, neighborhood
or part of town or country but
not in my back yard.

Today I Decide Not to Read about the Vanishing Snow Leopards

In late spring when the term ends on university campuses
animal-loving students release their cats into the natural world.
Wrens, robins, and warblers get jittery. Only the pesky starlings
appear to survive with ease in that suddenly perilous ecosystem.
Foreman of the ground crew says when they rounded up the felines
a few years back the mice and rats had a field-day, "went ape-shit."
Since then, they've "just let them do what cats will do."

In this morning's *Tribune* the mayor of Asotin, Washington,
complains of feral cats: "They always show up at dusk."
Nearly a dozen emerge from the shadows, dodging off
when a couple of kids whiz past on their clattering bikes.
The mayor sets a pair of traps baited with off-brand tuna.
"They ain't picky," she says, and sure enough, six hours later
she has herself a pair of tabbies, "wilder than March hares."
"Don't dare handle them without heavy leather gloves."
Takes them away to be spayed at the animal shelter.

Last month's Smithsonian magazine ran a cover
showing a pensive-looking snow leopard in Kyrgyzstan.
People, of course, are the real problem, gone soft-hearted
over unwanted pets that prove pricey to feed, and besides
the kids have decided they'd rather play videogames.
The smarter cats avoid the mayor of Asotin, who is not
at all clear on how she "got stuck with this job."
She laughs. "But someone's got to do it." Meanwhile,
the snow leopards are vanishing in Kyrgyzstan.

Vespula pensylvanica, the Western Yellowjacket

> *"If you encounter a yellow-jacket nest,
> contact a local pest control expert immediately."*

Amy, our crazy neighbor from across the street,
shows up with her broom to battle the yellowjackets.
She has designs on three papery gray nests
set in the ivy on our back deck where Tommy,
her teenaged son, has contracted to do some trimming.

We greet her at the driveway, me with my deadly
fourteen-ounce black can of wasp and hornet spray:
"Kills the entire nest!" "¡Mata el Nido Entero!"
Somehow, having it spelled out in two languages
enhances my confidence even more than the chemistry:
Prallethrin and Cypermethrin in such miniscule
percentages they challenge my faith in entomology.

I've used it before and can attest it lives up
to its fatal billing: "kills on contact instantly, sprays
up to twenty-two feet" (I've paced it off, not being one
to take chances when it comes to insecticide).

But crazy Amy came of age in a commune,
double-majored in communication and life
sciences, what in my day they called biology,
and here she comes with her blue-handled broom
like a pretty witch ready to sweep our ivy
clean of the nested yellowjackets so her boy can safely
collect a few sweaty dollars trimming the vines.

It's late afternoon of a day in the nineties.
She has it in mind that my can of lethal ingredients

topped with a black plastic cone to direct the spray
(I've seen these at the end of machinegun barrels)
may do irreparable harm to less threatening species:
bees and butterflies, lady bugs and what not,
common house flies, mosquitoes, and then perfectly
innocent and beneficent birds might perish utterly
in the aftermath of their insectious, dare I say, entrees.

Crazy Amy is not at all dressed for the job—
just shorts and a simple halter-top, no gloves,
not even a hat to keep the angry, unhoused vespides
out of her long brown hair, but she's intrepid,
there on her knees knocking off a pair
of nests and telling us to stay back just in case,
and I'm yelling at her uselessly to be careful
and reminding her these are not endangered species,
and the manufacturer of my product guarantees,
and I quote, they're "A Family Company."

Guided Tour of the Hemingway Home and Museum

> *Every poem an epitaph.*
> — T.S. Eliot

Maria, the deep-voiced guide at Hemingway's place in Key West,
spoke mostly out the corner of her mouth as if confiding in us,
as if imparting dark secrets Papa would prefer had stayed unsaid.

When she ushered us upstairs to gawk at Ernest and Pauline's bed,
one of the six-toed cats came along, a calico named Fred Astaire
I think, but I may have made that up. Their life was so confusing,

distorted out of its context, which is not to say it couldn't be amusing.
Consider the headboard of their nuptial bed, a gate procured,
Maria said, from some obscure monastic garden in Spain,

late Renaissance, note the craftsmanship for which Hem paid pesetas.
The Great Depression, after all, struck everywhere. Maria sighed
wistfully and tossed a mess of Friskies on the writer's bed,

and Fred seemed truly gratified. Yes, Papa loved his kotsies
and his dogs, Maria said. And Pauline loved her artsy chandeliers
and colorful Spanish tiles. We should watch for those. This house was hers.

A cast-iron catwalk used to join the second story to his writing studio
across the way. He'd write from six till noon. Later we could take a look.
His desk is there, some miscellaneous books, a few stuffed heads.

And here, Maria said, was Ernest's favorite place in the house, his toilet
looking out on Whitehead Street where he'd sit and try to think
and shout to passing friends and neighbors, ask them in for drinks.

Here's the steel helmet he wore in Italy on the very brink of death,
and here's the birthing chair he'd take for guests when deep-sea fishing,
and here's that urinal he brought home one afternoon from Sloppy Joe's.

Oh, Pauline didn't think too much of that, husky-voiced Maria said
but look here: still the largest private swimming pool in Key West.
It was salt-water, very fashionable then, and here is Papa's penny,
Hemingway's last red cent, Maria laughed. Pauline set it in cement.

Papa Visits the Key West Place

Always start out at the southernmost point on South.
Most tourists can't tell me from the lookalikes,
so I tell them I'm just passing through, which is one
unspeakably true sentence if there ever was one.

Try to drop by after the tourists are gone,
most of them plopping down at Sloppy Joe's
pretending to be me, as if all I ever did
was booze it up and flirt with gorgeous broads.

Always check on the kotsies and honestly
couldn't care less how many toes they have.
Neighbors used to complain about missing chicks,
but cats will be cats and dogs will be dogs.

Like to look in at the old master bedroom
half expecting to find Pauline there under that
damn chandelier ready to bitch me out, half
expecting to find Snowball curled up on the bed.

Always roost a few minutes there on the throne
overlooking Whitehead Street, brood a bit
the way anyone would do, great writer or not.
Best unprintable room in the house.

Get a rise out of Pauline's penny set in cement
by her damn swimming pool in which I always
take a quick piss, allow myself a minute to smile
at the tiles she slapped on Josie's old urinal.

Always wander across to the studio and sit
right there at the desk as if I could still do it.
You know what I mean, sit there and glare
at that sweet old Royal like a lost soul.

Find a Grave

Not there, despite the Frank Lloyd Wright
prairie-style homes, in Oak Park, Illinois,
outside Chicago where his mother
Grace held court.

Someone suggested the Upper Peninsula,
not Petoskey but north and west of there
near Seney and the Fox, or north of that
on some trout-rich branch of the Big Two-
Hearted where the burial
would not be tragic.

Of course, we thought of the Père Lachaise,
for him to be stretched out in the vicinity of Jim
Morrison, Molière, Edith Piaf, without regrets,
Chopin, Colette (they met once, he bought her
absinthe of course), Balzac, Bizet, Max Ernst
and you know who—Gertrude—to whom
he owed a debt or two.

Spain came to mind right away, perhaps Málaga
or Ronda, where villagers tossed the fascists
over the cliff, presumably even the priest,
or the corrida of San Fermín at Pamplona
or Madrid where he watched Lalanda,
Belmonte, El Gallo, Chicuelo, matadors
master the art of that murderous ballet
except poor Joselito.

Or what about Italy, you might ask, to be interred
on an isle in Venice, nel Cimitero di San Michele
in the neighborhood of Joe Brodsky, the Stravinskys,

little Igor and Vera, a stone's throw from Ezra Pound,
his old tennis partner. But wouldn't a site on the Piave
have made more sense, where his right leg and hip
were riddled by shrapnel from an Austrian
mortar shell?

Or how about Key West, a solemn cortege
of lookalikes to parade past his swimming pool
arriving at Sloppy Joe's in time for happy hour?
Bedroom just as he left it, Royal typewriter
at rest in his office across the catwalk
ready for one more true sentence. Later we may
scatter his ashes in the graveyard of those
anarchic six-toed cats.

Did we consider eastern Africa, some plot
under Kilimanjaro, Tanganyika as it was then?
Yes we did, but decided lions, hyenas, even rhinos,
impala, eland, oryx, kudo, that memorable old bull
might disturb his eternal rest in vengeance for his
pursuits "remembered," as the Masai say,
of the unforgetful elephant.

So, it came down at last to the Finca Vigía
near Havana, but think of the politics,
and a flat slab in Idaho shadowed by the raw
Sawtooths and showered with random coins.
Ketchum caught what was left of him "forever,"
as advertised by the bronze marker on Trail Creek,
leaves on the trout streams, "high blue
windless skies" overhead.

Citizens of the World

From Logan airport to his hotel in the Back Bay,
arriving late at night, the scholar grabs a cab
piloted by a tiny black woman from Uganda.
Her wrist is sprained, so she cannot manage
his hefty baggage. He resists asking her
about Idi Amin Dada, crocodiles
in the swimming pools, and the disaster that
calls itself South Sudan. He tips her
way too heavily to make up for everything.

The next day the cabbie who takes him to Cambridge
hails from Senegal and he struggles to recall
that famous West African poet, but fails,
suspects the guy would not have been impressed
anyway. Back at the hotel he looks it up:
Léopold Senghor, Senegal's first president,
served for twenty years, graduated the Sorbonne,
nearly executed by the Nazis, sage of Dakar.
He tips the cabbie extra to excuse his memory lapse.

The driver from Haiti on day three tells him
he's never going back. He mentions Papa Doc
but the cabbie, just a boy, knows nothing of him,
or even Baby Doc. He has not read that novel by
Graham Greene, did not see the movie with
Richard Burton and Elizabeth Taylor. The scholar
has a very nice voice, sings a few bars of
"Island in the Sun," imitation Harry Belafonte.
The cabbie shakes his head sadly.
At the end of this ride everyone feels guilty.

On Friday he takes the T and shuttle to the JFK
to do some research in the Hemingway collection.
In his letters to Martha, Hem calls her Bongie, and he
also calls himself Bongie, and he calls her Mookie,
also Pooky and Pickly, and he complains bitterly
about her absences and thyroid medication.
At the shuttle bus stop an old German
whose wild white hair blows about in the stiff
wind off the Atlantic asks the bus driver
how much for a taxi to Beacon Hill, but the driver
tells him to go back and ask at the desk. The scholar
could direct him to the T but doesn't,
not wanting to get involved.

The cabbie who hauls him back to Logan
early Monday morning comes from Ghana,
drove cabs six years in London, shows him
Tom Brady's chateau-style home on Commonwealth,
says his wife and three kids live out in Lynn, says
the Brits called it Gold Coast. He goes back home
every year. He cannot understand why Americans
don't know more of their own history, says
he cannot understand Nigeria, the universal corruption,
says as a boy he thought the streets of Boston
were probably paved in gold.

In October

Nicolaus Host (1761-1834), botanist

Ruthless today I shear away
yellowed hordes of slug-embattled Hosta,
remnants of summer's vegetation
once towering over the gold day lilies,
woolly thyme, primroses, hellebore.
Why, I wonder as I slash, do I take
such boyish pleasure in this act,
hacking them down four inches from the ground,
pitiless in my attack on their
doomed beauty? Why do I feel no mercy
wielding my shears, their nine-inch blades
paired Bowie knives carving
such bitter cuts, never having served,
never having seen the elephant of war?

My Brother's War

My brother suffered a little in boot camp
under the hard heel and bark
of a top sergeant who liked to shout,
"Clean up ever bit of der-bis
here on the parade ground, in the barracks,
in the parking lot, on the rifle range!"
He liked that word, "der-bis,"
and like all non-coms did not like
to be called "sir"
because, he said, he *worked* for a living.

My brother went on to Pleiku,
getting there just in time for Tet,
stopping at Tan San Nhut Airbase,
port of debarkation, to paint rocks.
"No such-a-thing," Tom quotes, "as a rock
that don't need another coat of paint."
Sergeant Price taught them that, too,
taught the boots how to paint rocks. White.
"White rocks," the sergeant said, "looks good."
Like Arlington, like those tombstones.

Sergeant Price, that war has ended.
That war is over now. That war,
unlike all those others, was not a good war.
That war bruised all of us, everyone,
but what war doesn't?
Sergeant Price,
long ago retired or dead,
another clump of der-bis, or debris, his war.

Lesson from the War: The Forgetting of Parts

This grainy gray-and-white snapshot
shows my younger brother Tom
smiling over the disassembled pieces
of his M-14 rifle as if to ask a bit
sheepishly whether anyone on God's
green earth or on this dusty orange
hill overlooking the city of Pleiku
has any vague notion how to reassemble
this damnable contraption in time
for inspection or the Tet Offensive,
which is just about to happen.

Back in Basic the top sergeant said
the hard part's putting it back together,
and the hard part's pulling the trigger
so you hit something in the vicinity of
what you might be aiming at, and
the hard part's aiming at something
worth aiming at, and the hard part's
keeping your cool and not burning
eighty rounds the first ten minutes.
Do you hear me? Yes, sergeant!
An unloaded rifle, he said, is called a club.

My brother is about to survive the war
unscathed, not scathed, not harmed,
from the Old Norse, my brother
the Viking warrior wearing oversized
olive drab fatigues and regulation
ball-cap and black-rimmed glasses
and smiling as he sits on a stack
of sandbags wondering where's the stock,

polished walnut, and where's the receiver
for that matter, or the four magazines
of shiny 7.62-millimeter cartridges
I had around here somewhere?

This ten-pound thing would make
a great club, he thinks, come the first
whump of the 81-millimeter mortar.
A couple of guys in his unit were not
so lucky, he would say years later.
Years later he would say if he could've just
put the damned thing back together,
we probably would've won the war.

Language Barriers

I want to write a poem about
what the hell has happened to the petals,
pink petals from our crabapple tree,
and I want to write the same poem about
what the hell has happened
to Russia since I took classes in Russian
and fell in love with Lermontov
sixty years ago.

This happened in Cocoa, Florida,
Saltwater Trout Capital of the World
and host city to Brevard Junior College
and Cape Canaveral,
where we Americans chased after Sputnik
which distorted and metamorphosed itself
somehow into Putin.
But let's get back to crabapples.

These wilted petals on our patio
browning underfoot after an early June
downpour that ripped them
from their green leafy comfort
disturb me with thoughts of time and death
and how human behavior and history
imitate change and Crimea.
I liked the Russian language right off

despite the messy verbs, especially the verbs
of going and coming and going away again,
and while I never approached fluency,
I learned a lot about the people
(I thought) and Chekhov.

Those who know say Ukrainian
sounds almost the same, but Ukrainians
claim a different mother tongue.

Poems for "The Hurting Kind"

*Ada Limon at the Art Spirit Gallery,
Coeur d'Alene, Idaho, April 21, 2023*

People on the sidewalk keep walking by
looking through the windows, drawn
to the light, so many casual moths
wondering what's going on inside,
disinclined to enter

where the national poet laureate
in her nondescript pale blue dress,
elegantly simple and simply elegant,
almost sings as she
spins her words

for us to take or leave, to make whatever
we wish to make of them, for poets
make word gadgets, fragments that need
readers or listeners like us to complete.
She needs us.

She's shorter than I imagined from photos
in her half dozen books, first time in Idaho,
and looks, as folks around here might say,
"more Mexican," by which they mostly mean
"illegal immigrant."

Halfway through, a burly young man
glowers into our bright art gallery,
his cheeks burning, but his girlfriend
takes him by the arm and leads him
back into the shadows.

Within the gallery's silence
our national poet twitches her soft
blue dress and smiles, tells us she's
"doing what she can to survive," she's
"simply making music."

Marking Papers While Watching a Baseball Game

Glancing up from marking a misplaced modifier,
the prof watches his son slide headfirst into third.
His wife leaps from her bleacher seat
shrieking like a banshee as he
quietly strikes out a misspelled word.

Context is all. Near the end of the next inning
their son strikes out and in the next
commits an error about the time
the prof crosses off a homophonic flaw:
"there's" for "theirs."
                           But in the fifth
his boy draws a walk and steals second,
dusts himself off like a major leaguer,
spits a spray of sunflower hulls at the bag.

The prof's about to lay into a noun-pronoun
agreement error when their son
gets tagged out trying to come home.
His wife showers him with peanut shells,
scolds him for not focusing on the game.

In the seventh their son snares a liner
just as the professor lights with malicious glee
into a misapplied semi-colon.
Will their son knock in the walk-off run?
Will the prof see it if he does, or will he
suddenly discover yet another error, a
perilously run-on sentence?

IV.

Don't Feed the Bears

In this dream he did indeed go out to the woods alone,
uncompanioned by anyone who could be his brother,
his old friend Steve, and yes, he was in for a big surprise
because there in the knee-high huckleberries
two black bear cubs were feeding along like a pair
of oblivious pigs. He had not, as the old song advises,
thought to wear a disguise, or even to carry a gun.

He knew he should stop because their ursine mother
would surely be nearby, but common sense
rarely played a major part in his dreams,
so he blundered along and the hungry cubs
ignored him, as children will do when it comes to
adult interlopers clearly out of their proper element.

But suddenly, as in a Dostoevsky novel,
out of nowhere to his right and slightly behind,
came the sow with a low, predictable growl,
or maybe a grunt of grizzly disapprobation,
reminding him of the professor he was,
even in sleep, and that line from Chekhov's
Three Sisters came to mind: "He had no time
to say alack before the bear was on his back!"
Proverbial. Captain Solyony, Russian for "salty."

But in a potential nightmare involving a large,
perturbed bear, who has time to wax literary?
So, feeling very much an endangered species,
he reached over her heavy head and stroked her,
petted her dark fur as if she were nothing
more perilous than his daughter's declawed kitten,
the urbane Benson, a very civil cat indeed,

not inclined to bite even the hand that does not
feed her, and the great bear nearly purred,
and he woke up stroking his wife's bright hair.

The Lover of Lakes

"Lakes are my love," she says, "lakes
are my love." Meaning, I think, not me,
having almost drowned in several
various lakes from Florida to Washington.
I could swim and nearly drown my way
diagonally across this great nation.

When my family moved to watery Florida,
my father wanted me to learn to swim
pronto, my mother being a noted Ohio
hydrophobe.
              And so one afternoon
at a place incongruously named Dinky Dock,
eight years old and in love, I think,
with a freckle-faced girl named Mimi
who wore a blue-and-white polka dot suit
trimmed with white ruffles at the top,
I almost drowned for the first time.

A few years later, at Camp La-No-Che,
near Paisley, I regaled my Boy Scout buddies
with an underwater reprise,
me submersible
              dog-paddling about
halfway to the Swimming merit badge and back.

Later still I swam for the CHS swim team,
four hundred meter very freestyle,
my goal being not to drown, my goal
being to beat my own best time,
ten minutes more or less,
                    and to win

at least one point for the team by default,
which would happen only if I remained afloat.

Now she shows me her favorite girlhood lake,
points to a boulder a hundred yards away in the sun,
and strokes to it seamless in her wine-dark suit.
We're in Idaho now and I know I could drown
over this kind of lacustrine love.

Arachnophilia

Miss Muffett, my wife opines, was no fool,
and if, as some scientists now say,
spiders dream, their much-loved nightmares
surely would frighten Georgia away.

Last night I dabbed pricey Clobetasol
to nine bites about her body: lower back,
inside left elbow, nape of her sweet neck,
six tiny blisters on her right forearm,

perhaps the sequential nips of a single
irked arachnid in search of some more suitable
nourishment—a common housefly, moth, or bee.
Why do they find Georgia so delectable?

Both of us had spent the past four days
scraping and painting our resurrected deck,
nurturing dreams of evening parties, wine,
soft music, occasionally enlightened talk,

not dreaming of whatever dark hunger drives
some spiders to dream of juicy human flesh.
And why, if these noiseless, patient spiders must
feast at times on the human beast, why not on me?

At the Speed of Love

No love runs as fast as this
American love of now.
It flies from underfoot,
like a startled cock pheasant
or a covey of flushed quail
whirring away from your shot
heartbreakingly beautiful
in their sudden feathery death.
In this country love
rarely lasts a season
before it morphs into
something unpredictable,
at once particle and wave.
You can't keep up with it.

A Lover's Game

Georgia taught me how to loop the string
meaningfully so it would, as she put it,
"come to something" in my clumsy fingers.

Before she came along, I suspected I was
just tying myself into knots, some random,
some in my confusion thoroughly Gordian.

"Do it like this," she said, her slender fingers
educated at the Steinway. She meant
for us to share the artistry of it, the intent.

Eiffel Tower, Cat's Eye, Fish in a Dish, so many
figures, more than twenty thousand in twenty
or so minutes according to the Guinness book.

"Look," Georgia whispered, "Jacob's Ladder,
Ace of Diamonds, Many Stars, Broken Heart."
I couldn't help falling in love with her.

That's when she taught me so many versions
that can be played alone, Cat's Cradle solitaire
for when it happened she might not be there.

The Photographer & the Angler

On this bridge over this small stream,
she struggles to snap, if that's the right
verb, a photograph of an old angler
disturbing the air with his fly line.
She has just happened upon this guy
in his blue flannel shirt and black cap
assaulting the sky with his yellow line
in the off chance a cutthroat trout
might strike that brown-and-white tuft
tied to the end of a tiny, brightly gilded
hook.   Although, speaking realistically,
most of that comes to more than she knows.
What she knows is this old angler
resembles her father on his better days,
which happened only in her imagination.
Her father was the sort of fisherman
best left to himself on some distant
stream where he could not hurt anyone.

Aquariums

As a child she had goldfish
her father told her were meant
to teach her responsibility.
She must feed them carefully,
not too much, not too little.

When she was a girl her mother,
single by then, bought her colorful
tropical fish and a warm
saltwater aquarium.
An aerator bubbled all the time.
All the girl had to do was keep
the tank clean. This would teach her
to take care of herself.

Her husband did not like fish.
No aquariums in his house.
He kept a pair of German shorthairs.
This would teach her obedience.

When she got old and lived alone,
she kept a Japanese geisha doll
under a glass case.
"Look," she told her grown daughters,
"look at all I've learned."

Amish Furniture in Sequim, Washington

(pronounced "skwim")

We almost bought a clock in Sequim,
and we almost bought an Amish dinner set,
eight chairs and a table with leaves
handmade maple from Indiana
where my wife once lived.

That Amish furniture brought us back
to a store in Sugarcreek, Ohio, and to the horse
auction at Kidron when Mom and Dad
were alive and my brother Dan
knew the back roads where the Amish
steered their buggies and we tried
to get the adults to smile without success.

We could not keep our hands off those
lustrous fabrics: walnut, cedar, cherry,
white and red oak, sapwood hickory,
heartwood. The plain elegance,
the unique grains, the children
glad to leave school after eighth grade,
quiet girls, modest wives and husbands.

Stroking the satin surface of one costly table,
we thought of a painting we bought Mom and Dad
ten years past in Pennsylvania, a primitive
oil of a yellow, one-room schoolhouse
featuring sixteen children at recess
swinging, jumping rope, playing tag, two

black-hat boys pulling their black-bonnet sisters
in red wagons, and another boy
emerging from the outhouse, only his
black hat visible. The schoolmarm sweeps the porch.
In this simple painting by Dolores Hackenberger,
no features appear on any face, not so much
as an eye, or a nose, or a smile.

But we could not afford that Amish furniture,
trees some nameless craftsman transfigured
into hardwood art, into full-grained poetry.
As with a Van Gogh or an Edward Hopper,
we could only admire the quiet genius.

Romance on the Patio

— for Georgia

"I don't know. Goldfinches maybe."
He's asked her favorite songbird
and when she looks up, four of them,
goldfinches, sip at the copper
birdbath seemingly taking turns.
How can she not admire them,
such polite birds?

"I love nuthatches," he says, not
because he's thought about it but because
a pair of them have just now perched
on her recently replenished feeder
seemingly polite and fastidious
in their pecking, not making a mess.
He loves this woman.

Backyard Bird Count

Following that seven-thirty flurry of birds
nothing, not so much as a ragged sparrow.

We're half listening to a classical music channel,
Beethoven's fifth violin sonata, "Spring,"

even though it's only two-thirds into February,
so we're being teased and we know it.

The online weather report for tomorrow threatens
snow by way of reprimanding us for

yet another tour-de-force in self-delusion.
Local papers have ceased deliveries

leaving us vulnerable to the vagaries of
television and online news when it comes

to keeping up with various wars and assorted
calamities. We're both of us past eighty,

that time of life when one must rely on birds
or poetry for the really important news.

Poetry is news that stays news.
— Ezra Pound (1934)

About the Author

Ron McFarland was born in Bellaire, Ohio, grew up in Cocoa, Florida, took his bachelor's and master's degrees in English from Florida State University in Tallahassee, taught two years at Sam Houston State in Huntsville, Texas, garnered his doctorate at the University of Illinois with a dissertation in 17th-century British literature, and embarked on a nearly 50-year teaching career at the University of Idaho, where he acted as impresario of poetry readings, served for many years as faculty advisor of the literary magazine *Fugue,* and helped create the MFA program. He played soccer with the Idaho club team for more than twenty years.

He was an Eagle Scout, and he played trumpet in a very good high school band. He almost played on the baseball team at Brevard Junior College (now East Florida State College), but instead edited the school newspaper, which prompted him to be a writer. He worked as library assistant in the Cocoa Public Library. In Texas he and a colleague edited a freshman composition reader-rhetoric, *American Controversy,* published by Scott-Foresman in 1968—his first book.

Confluence Press (Lewiston, Idaho) published a chapbook of his poems, *Certain Women,* in 1977, and he edited an anthology, *Eight Idaho Poets,* published by the University Press of Idaho. In 1984 he was named the state's first Writer-in-Residence, a two-year position that entailed giving ten readings a year throughout the state for the next two years. In that context Confluence published his first full-length book of poems, *Composting at Forty*. His thirty-odd books include chapbooks of poems and booklets in the Western Writers Series on Tess Gallagher, William Kittredge, and Norman Maclean. The University of Idaho Press published his *The World of David Wagoner* in 1997.

Ron's new and selected poems, *Stranger in Town,* appeared in 2000, the year Permafrost Press released his chapbook, *The Mad Waitress Poems*. His most recent full-length collection of poems, *Subtle Thieves,* appeared in 2012. Other titles include a memoir of growing up in Florida during the 1950s & 1960s, *Confessions of a Night Librarian and Other Embarrassments, Catching First Light* (stories & essays from Idaho), *The Rockies in First Person* (a study of regional memoirs), *Appropriating Hemingway: Using Him as a Fictional Character, Edward J. Steptoe and the Indian Wars* and most recently, *Gary Soto: A Career in Poetry and Prose* (2022) and *Professor McFarland in Reel Time: Poems and Prose of an Angler* (2020).

His two grown daughters and son have provided him with five grandchildren. With the love of his life Georgia Tiffany, pianist, former high school teacher, and poet, he has acquired four additional grandchildren. Georgia's first full-length collection of poems, *Body Be Sound,* has just been published by Encircle Press. An occasional bird hunter, he regards himself as an avid but mostly inept fly angler. He currently serves as program director of the Clearwater Fly Casters.

About Cirque Press

Cirque Press grew out of *Cirque,* a literary journal that publishes the works of writers and artists from the North Pacific Rim, a region that reaches north from Oregon to the Yukon Territory, south through Alaska to Hawaii, and west to the Russian Far East.

Cirque Press is a partnership of Sandra Kleven, publisher, and Michael Burwell, editor. Ten years ago, we recognized that works of talented writers in the region were going unpublished, and the Press was launched to bring those works to fruition. We publish fiction, nonfiction, and poetry, and we seek to produce art that provides a deeper understanding about the region and its cultures. The writing of our authors is significant, personal, and strong.

Sandra Kleven — Michael Burwell, publishers and editors

www.cirquejournal.com

Books from Cirque Press

Apportioning the Light by Karen Tschannen (2018)
The Lure of Impermanence by Carey Taylor (2018)
Echolocation by Kristin Berger (2018)
Like Painted Kites & Collected Works by Clifton Bates (2019)
Athabaskan Fractal: Poems of the Far North
    by Karla Linn Merrifield (2019)
Holy Ghost Town by Tim Sherry (2019)
Drunk on Love: Twelve Stories to Savor Responsibly
    by Kerry Dean Feldman (2019)
Wide Open Eyes: Surfacing from Vietnam by Paul Kirk Haeder (2020)
Silty Water People by Vivian Faith Prescott (2020)
Life Revised by Leah Stenson (2020)
Oasis Earth: Planet in Peril by Rick Steiner (2020)
The Way to Gaamaak Cove by Doug Pope (2020)
Loggers Don't Make Love by Dave Rowan (2020)
The Dream That Is Childhood by Sandra Wassilie (2020)
Seward Soundboard by Sean Ulman (2020)
The Fox Boy by Gretchen Brinck (2021)
Lily Is Leaving: Poems by Leslie Ann Fried (2021)
One Headlight by Matt Caprioli (2021)
November Reconsidered by Marc Janssen (2021)
Callie Comes of Age by Dale Champlin (2021)
Someday I'll Miss This Place Too by Dan Branch (2021)
Out There In The Out There by Jerry McDonnell (2021)
Fish the Dead Water Hard by Eric Heyne (2021)
Salt & Roses by Buffy McKay (2022)
Growing Older In This Place: A Life in Alaska's Rainforest
    by Margo Wasserman Waring (2022)
Kettle Dance: A Big Sky Murder by Kerry Dean Feldman (2022)
Nothing Got Broke by Larry F. Slonaker (2022)
On the Beach: Poems 2016-2021 by Alan Weltzien (2022)
Sky Changes on the Kuskokwim by Clifton Bates (2022)

Transplanted By Birgit Lennertz Sarrimanolis (2022)
Between Promise and Sadness by Joanne Townsend (2022)
Yosemite Dawning by Shauna Potocky (2022)
The Woman Within by Tami Phelps and Kerry Dean Feldman (2023)
In the Winter of the Orange Snow by Diane S. Carpenter (2023)
Mail Order Nurse by Sue Lium (2023)
All in Due Time by Kate Troll (2023)
Infinite Meditations For Inspiration and Daily Practice
    by Scott Hanson (2023)
Getting Home from Here by Anne Ward-Masterson (2023)
Crossing the Burnside Bridge & Other Poems by Janice D. Rubin (2023)
A Variable Sense of Things by Ron McFarland (2023)
May the Owl Call Again: A Return to Poet John Meade Haines,
    1924-2011 by Rachel Epstein (2024)
Tiny's Stories: An Athabascan Family on the Yukon River
    by Theresa "Tiny" Demientieff Devlin with Sam Demientieff (2024)
If Singing Went On by Gerald Cable (2024)
Out of the Dark: A Memoir by Marian Elliott (2024)

CIRCLES
Illustrated books from Cirque Press

Baby Abe: A Lullaby for Lincoln by Ann Chandonnet (2021)
Miss Tami, Is Today Tomorrow? by Tami Phelps (2021)
Miss Bebe Goes to America by Lynda Humphrey (2022)

More Praise for *A Variable Sense of Things*

What a delightful and surprising late-career gift from Ron McFarland. The trademark McFarland insouciance and humor are displayed in abundance, but also a reflectiveness, a tenderness. These poems look back more than forward, and they do so thoughtfully and appreciatively toward a life robustly lived, with octogenarian wiliness and even a bit of wisdom. *A Variable Sense of Things* is among the very best work of a poet who has charmed us for decades.

> — **Gaylord Brewer**, author of *Country of Ghost* and *Worship the Pig*

A Variable Sense of Things is a book of poems by Ron McFarland that begins with a lovely prayer for the optimism of seeds that regenerate up from Americana dirt. We are led from "the small town anywhere" that we left for good. Childhood, school, snapshots of those we knew, those we were, in a succession of nowhere jobs—the customer service representative, the Polish immigrant's grocery store, and romance of logging. We see it up close, are the also-rans. We came in second in the piano competition, only placed in the swim meet. We think about our weight, are proud of our fingernails, are proud of our dangerous jobs at the coal mine and at pulling green chain. We sleep above the store. For us, the immigrants, this feels like safety. Grown men with the mind of teenagers after work beer their way to a place with loud music but sadly without a cheerleader in the joint. And yet in this garden of growth, death, and renewal there is love as common as goldfinches at the feeder and a wife teaching your fingers Cat's Cradle.

> — **David McElroy**, author of *Just Between Us* and *Water The Rocks Make*

Poems by Ohio born, Florida raised, now Idaho Professor Emeritus Ron McFarland offer stunning snapshots of this land and nation, and the moments we all know as "life lived." From 23 literary journals he offers 64 delightful poems about *A Variable Sense of Things*, from manatees and birds to the lessons of grade school days, from Hemingway to loggers and librarians. Agreeing with Ezra pound that "Poetry is news that stays news," Ron ends by observing he's reached "that time of life when one must rely on birds / or poetry for the really important news."

> — **Kerry Dean Feldman**, author of *Alice's Trading Post: A Novel of the West* and co-author of *The Woman Within: Memory as Muse*

www.ingramcontent.com/pod-product-compliance
Lightning Source LLC
Chambersburg PA
CBHW031128080526
44587CB00011B/1148